P9-CLE-654

DISCARD

For Dave

Mapping Sam
Copyright © 2018 by Joyce Hesselberth
All rights reserved. Printed in the United States of America.
For information address HarperCollins Children's Books,
a division of HarperCollins Publishers, 195 Broadway,
New York, NY 10007.
www.harpercollinschildrens.com

Watercolor, acrylic paint, gouache, and digital collage were used
to create the illustrations.
The text type is Clarendon.

Library of Congress Cataloging-in-Publication Data is available.
ISBN 978-0-06-274122-6 (hardback)

18 19 20 21 22 PC 10 9 8 7 6 5 4 3 2
First Edition

Greenwillow Books

MAPPING
SAM

Joyce Hesselberth

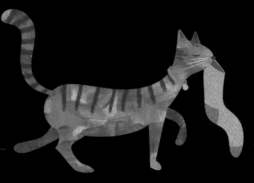

Greenwillow Books
An Imprint of HarperCollinsPublishers

Every night, Sam puts
her family to bed.

R0453880398

Once everyone is sound asleep,

Sam slips out the back door,
circles twice around the house,
and disappears into the darkness.

Where cats go at night is a bit of a mystery.
Let's see where Sam goes.

She leaps over a tall fence.

She sneaks through the wet grass.

She rolls across the neighbor's yard,
and almost catches her tail.

She climbs her favorite tree.

If we mapped the first part of Sam's journey, it would look like this.

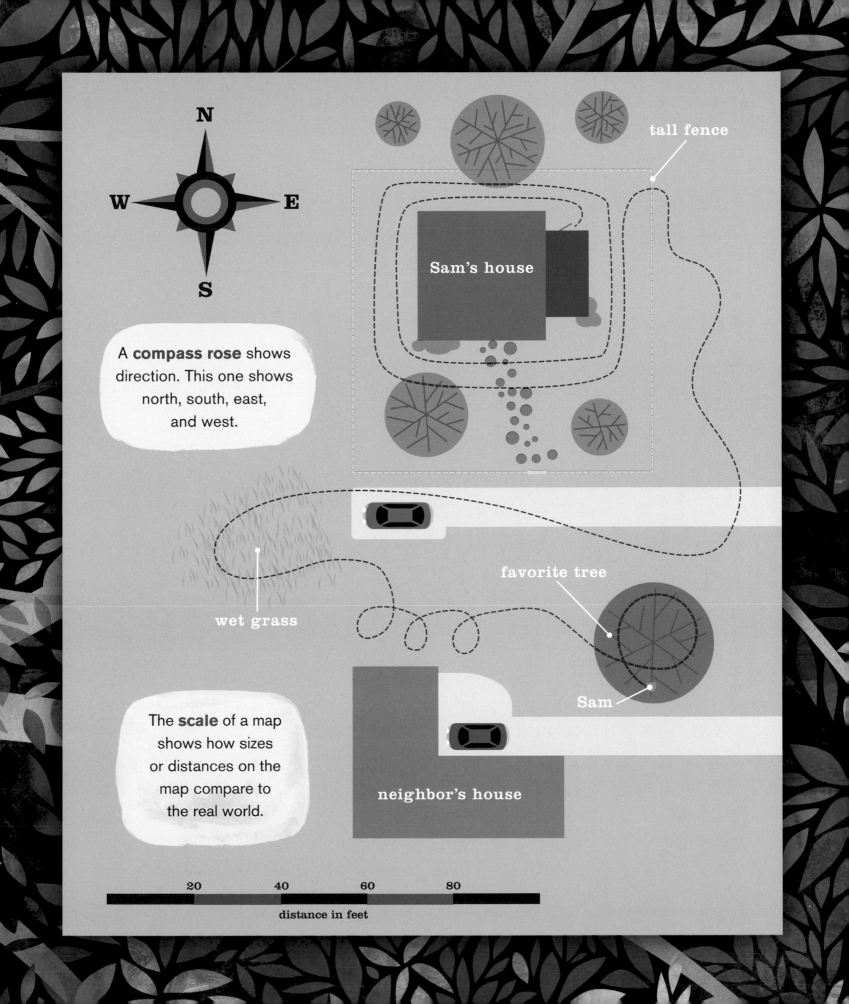

N

W E

S

tall fence

Sam's house

A **compass rose** shows direction. This one shows north, south, east, and west.

favorite tree

wet grass

Sam

The **scale** of a map shows how sizes or distances on the map compare to the real world.

neighbor's house

20   40   60   80

distance in feet

We can map lots of other things, too.
This is a map of Sam.

bladder colon spine spleen kidney

tail

small
intestine

back leg

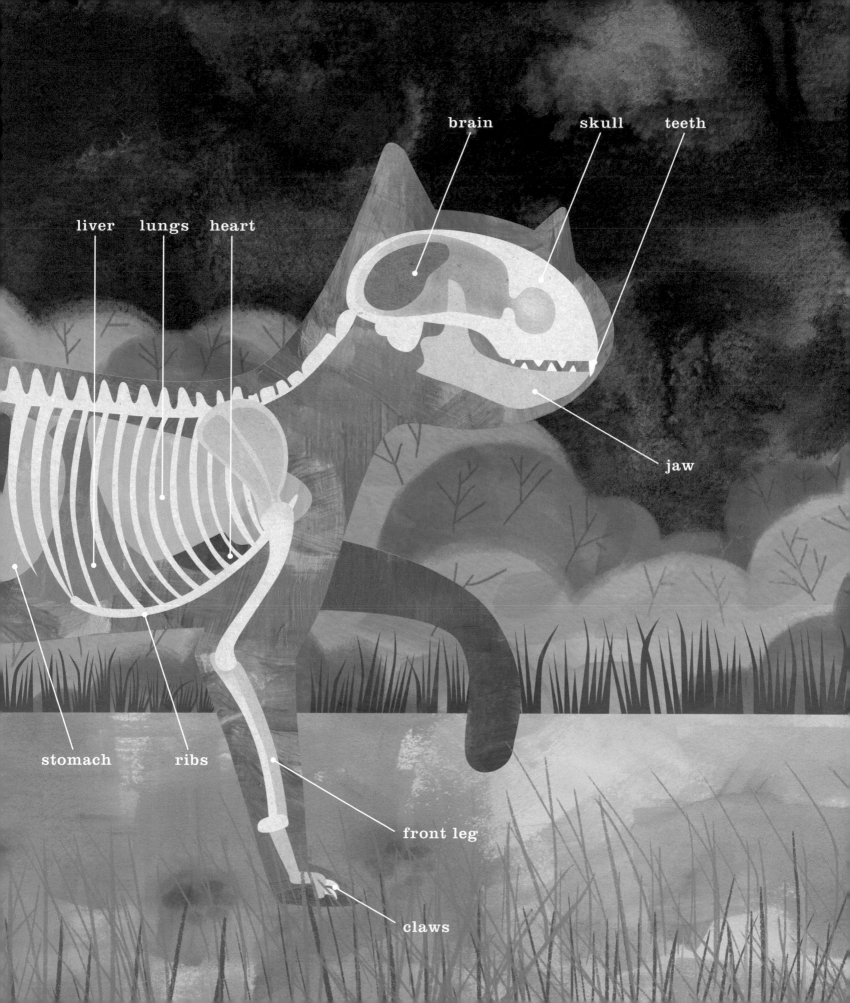

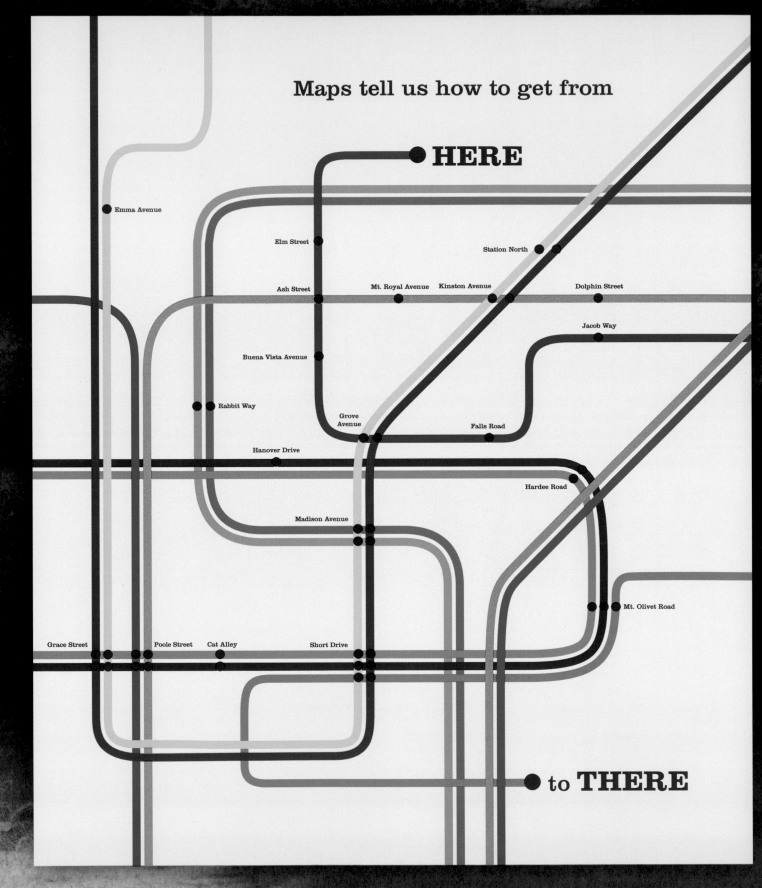

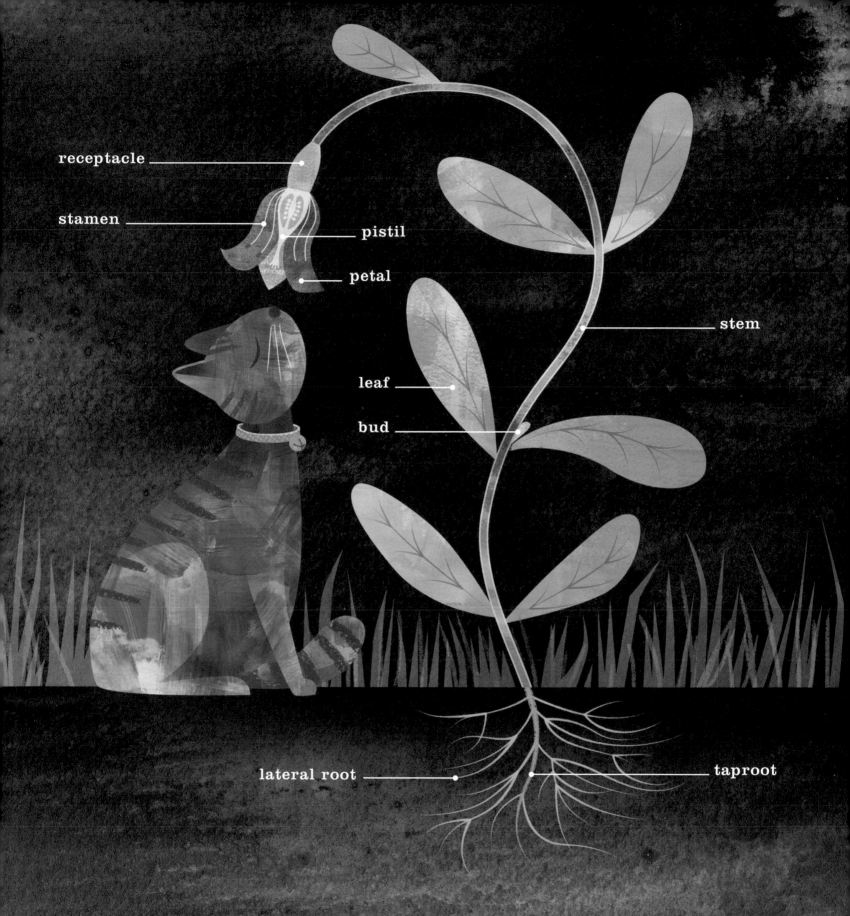

receptacle

stamen

pistil

petal

stem

leaf

bud

lateral root

taproot

Maps can also tell us what is where.

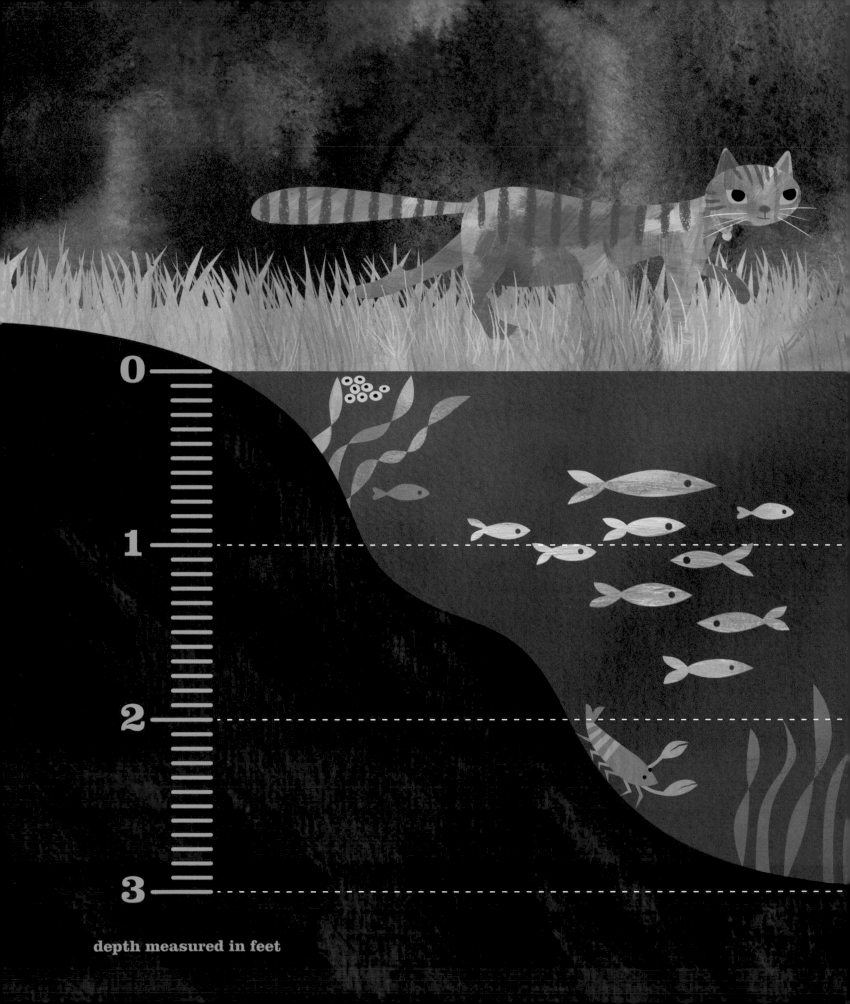

0

1

2

3

depth measured in feet

Maps can even show things
that you would normally never see,
like what is hidden in a pond . . .

or things that are
too small to see,
like a molecule
of water.

WATER MOLECULE

A water molecule is made of two hydrogen atoms and one oxygen atom.

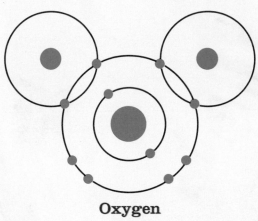

Hydrogen   **Hydrogen**

Oxygen

There are many, many water molecules in a single drop of water.

Europe

Asia

Africa

PACIFIC

OCEAN

INDIAN

OCEAN

Australia

**Maps can show things that are
big, like the Earth . . .**

Antarctica

or even bigger, like the planets
in our solar system.

SUN

Mercury

Venus

Earth

Mars

Sam

Jupiter

Saturn

Uranus

Neptune

Sam looks into the night sky.
People (and possibly cats) have
been reading the stars like
a map for thousands of years.

URSA MINOR

URSA MAJOR

VIRGO

LEO

By charting the stars, ship
captains could navigate the
oceans and travel the world.
Sam might travel someday.

GEMINI

CANCER

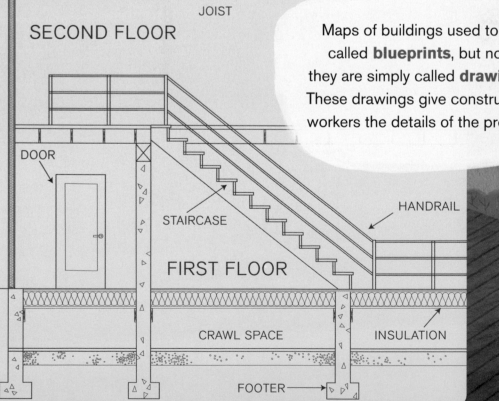

JOIST

SECOND FLOOR

DOOR

STAIRCASE

HANDRAIL

FIRST FLOOR

CRAWL SPACE

INSULATION

FOOTER

Maps of buildings used to be called **blueprints**, but now they are simply called **drawings**. These drawings give construction workers the details of the project.

But for right now, Sam wants to stay closer to home, and prefers her favorite lookout spot, on top of the (soon-to-be) tallest building in town. From up here, she can see the whole neighborhood.

Sam

And when Sam is sure that everything
in town is as it should be, she leaves her
perch, and heads for home . . .

where she creeps inside, and softly
pads up the stairs to fall asleep and
dream beautiful dreams.

Can you map a dream?
You might try.

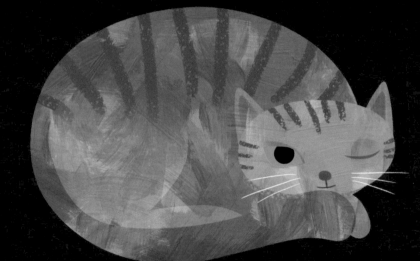

Good night, Sam.

Mapping Sam's World

A map is a picture, usually on a flat surface, that shows what is where and how to get from here to there. Maps can show things that are two-dimensional (flat) or three-dimensional (not flat). They can show things that are real (your town) or imaginary (a pretend kingdom). Some maps show distances, or illustrate how tall or deep things are. Other maps show how ideas are connected or how things work. Charts, graphs, diagrams, drawings, and patterns are all types of maps.

A mapmaker, also called a cartographer, is someone who makes maps. Mapmakers often show new or uncharted places in ways that help people understand, imagine, or travel in them.

This map shows Sam's route when she first leaves her house. It is a view from above. By using the compass rose and the scale on this page, you can figure out the directions that Sam travels and how far she goes.

This map shows the inside of Sam's body. You can use it to imagine Sam's skeleton and figure out where her major organs are (such as her heart).

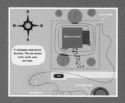

This is a transportation map showing many different color-coded lines (routes) and stops (stations). Can you map a route from Cat Alley to Rabbit Way?

This map is a botanical diagram. It shows the locations of the different parts of a plant and the way they are connected.

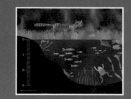

This cutaway map charts the depth of Sam's neighborhood pond and shows what she might see if there were a window in the side of the pond.

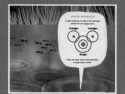

This map is a diagram of a water molecule, which is so small that it's invisible to your eye. It shows the even smaller pieces inside the molecule—the tiny building blocks called atoms. Look at a drop of water. That drop is made of billions of molecules.

This map shows what our planet would look like if it were stretched out flat. The equator cuts the earth in half. Longitude lines (east/west) and latitude lines (north/south) form a grid and help us navigate.

This map, a diagram of space, shows the sun and the position of the planets that form our solar system.

A map of the stars is called a constellation chart. People have often imagined pictures in the sky by drawing imaginary lines between stars. These pictures make groups of stars called constellations. Can you spot Ursa Major, also called the Big Dipper?

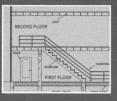

A blueprint is a guide or pattern that shows details, measurements, and layout for building something. By following the directions on this kind of map, builders construct things that work (such as cars) and buildings that don't tip over or leak or fall down.